PLACE GRANDCHILD'S PHOTO HERE.

BABY'S NAME: _____

BORN ON: <u>Sunday, October 18, 2020</u>

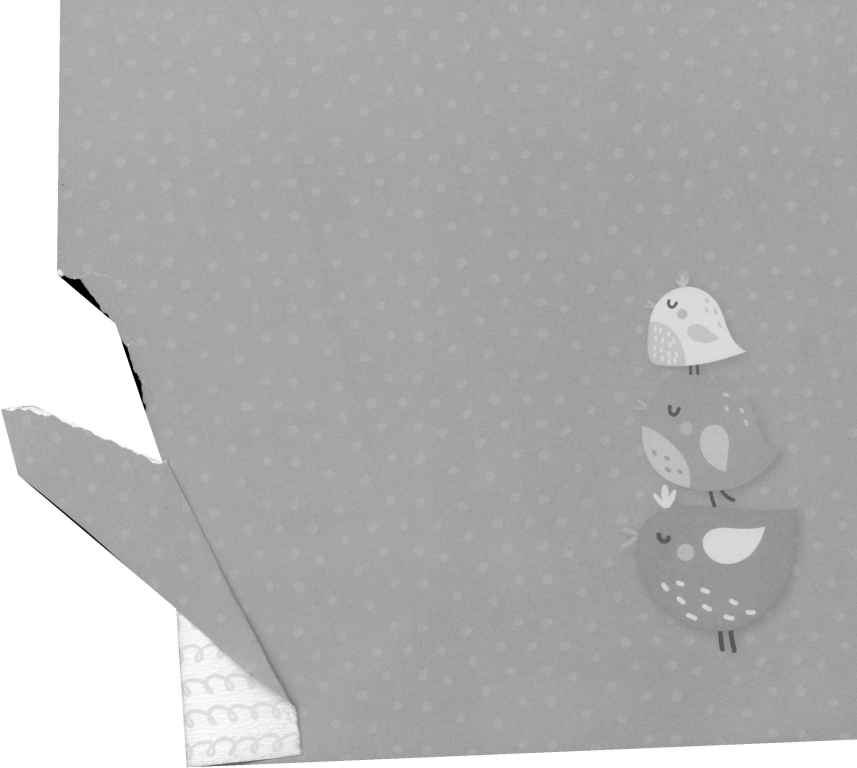

• A •
GRANDPARENT'S
KEEPSAKE ALBUM

SPECIAL MEMORIES OF
MY GRANDCHILD'S FIRST YEARS

LARK
New York

New York

An Imprint of Sterling Publishing Co., Inc.
1166 Avenue of the Americas
New York, NY 10036

ISBN 978-1-4547-1090-5

Distributed in Canada by Sterling Publishing Co., Inc.
c/o Canadian Manda Group, 664 Annette Street
Toronto, Ontario M6S 2C8, Canada
Distributed in the United Kingdom by GMC Distribution Services
Castle Place, 166 High Street, Lewes, East Sussex BN7 1XU, England
Distributed in Australia by NewSouth Books
University of New South Wales, Sydney, NSW 2052, Australia

For information about custom editions, special sales, and premium and corporate
purchases, please contact Sterling Special Sales at 800-805-5489
or specialsales@sterlingpublishing.com.

Manufactured in China

2 4 6 8 10 9 7 5 3

sterlingpublishing.com
larkcrafts.com

Interior design by Shannon Nicole Plunkett
Cover design by Elizabeth Mihaltse Lindy

All illustrations from Shutterstock.com by Nadezda Barkova and/or Kaliaha Volha

CAPTURE THE MEMORIES OF YOUR GRANDCHILD'S FIRST YEARS

The arrival of a grandchild is a special event for a family. While baby is busy bonding with her parents, she is also forming important relationships with other members of the family—siblings, aunts, uncles, and especially grandparents! Few relationships are as full of unconditional, pure love as the one between grandparent and grandchild. Whether you live in the next town or across the ocean, your grandchild can count on you for wisdom, encouragement, silliness, and lots of (virtual or in-person) hugs and kisses. From learning the news of baby's arrival to your first time babysitting to special ceremonies and outings, every moment with your new grandchild is a chance to build one of the most important relationships in both of your lives. You become part of baby's story—a story you'll want to chronicle and cherish as your grandchild grows.

A GRANDPARENT'S KEEPSAKE ALBUM—part journal, part photo album, part family heirloom—provides a way to organize and save all those photographs, invitations, and memorabilia. Here you'll chronicle those fleeting baby "firsts" and special moments between grandparent and grandchild, from the first time you give baby a bath to the first sleepover at your home to your first Mother's or Father's Day as a grandparent. You'll find space to record the names your grandchild called you, books you read together, lullabies you sang, funny things your grandchild said, and more. Within these pages, you can document the milestones in your new grandchild's life, as seen through your eyes.

With plenty of space for photos and mementos, this precious book will be a beloved keepsake to share as your grandchild grows, and to pass down from generation to generation.

PLACE PHOTO OF GRANDPARENTS HERE.

OUR MEMORIES OF YOU!

Welcome to the world, dear grandchild!

This first year—and those that follow—will be filled with so much wonder and joy. We're excited to begin this journey together, to capture the precious moments we share, and to one day share these special memories with you. Inside this volume we've collected our thoughts as we anticipated your arrival, reflections on our first moments and experiences together, stories of celebrations and gatherings, and *lots* of photographs and memorabilia. Your arrival marks the beginning of a wondrous new adventure. Inside these pages is our part of your unique and beautiful story.

◦ YOUR FAMILY TREE ◦

There's nothing more important than family—especially one as special as yours!
Here is a family tree of your parents, grandparents, and other relatives.

🍃 GREAT-GRANDPARENTS

_____

_____

🍃 GRANDPARENTS

_____

_____

🍃 GREAT-GRANDPARENTS

_____

_____

🍃 GREAT-GRANDPARENTS

_____

_____

🍃 GRANDPARENTS

_____

🍃 GREAT-GRANDPARENTS

_____

_____

PARENTS

_____

_____

YOU!

_____

SIBLINGS

_____

_____

9

COMING SOON

When we heard that you were on your way, we knew we were going to start an incredible adventure.

HERE'S HOW WE LEARNED THE WONDERFUL NEWS:

_____

_____

_____

_____

HERE'S HOW WE REACTED:

_____

_____

_____

_____

A SNEAK PEEK!

PLACE ULTRASOUND PHOTO HERE.

A LETTER TO YOUR PARENTS

Something wonderful happens when you become a grandparent—
your children become parents. Here are our words of wisdom to our
children as they become parents—the wonders we hope they experience,
the pitfalls we hope they avoid, and all the fun we hope they have!

_____

_____

_____

_____

_____

_____

_____

_____

_____

_____

_____

A LETTER TO YOU BEFORE YOU'RE BORN

We have so many hopes, dreams, and plans for us!
Here's what your arrival will mean to us, places we hope to go together,
things we'd like to teach you, and more.

_____

_____

_____

_____

_____

_____

_____

_____

_____

_____

_____

• PEARLS OF WISDOM •

Becoming a grandparent begins a new journey.
Here is a collection of the best advice we've received about becoming grandparents.

ADVICE:

_____

_____

_____

From _____

ADVICE:

_____

_____

_____

From _____

ADVICE:

_____

_____

_____

From _____

A SPECIAL INVITATION . . .

PLACE BABY SHOWER
INVITATION HERE.

PLACE BABY SHOWER PHOTOS HERE.

HERE ARE SOME SPECIAL GIFTS YOU RECEIVED:

_____

_____

_____

YOUR PARENTS WERE FEELING:

_____

_____

_____

YOUR GRANDPARENTS WERE FEELING:

_____

_____

_____

A SPECIAL MEMORY FROM YOUR SHOWER:

_____

_____

_____

HOW WE LEARNED OF YOUR ARRIVAL

We'll never forget the moment we found out that our special new grandchild was here!
Here's how we learned the joyful news!

_____

_____

_____

_____

_____

_____

_____

_____

_____

_____

_____

_____

PLACE BIRTH ANNOUNCEMENT HERE.

PLACE NEWSPAPER CLIPPINGS HERE.

PLACE PHOTOS OF YOU AND
THE NEWBORN HERE.

Here are some photos of your wonderful parents
during your newborn days.

PLACE PHOTOS OF THE PARENTS HERE.

• DON'T FORGET YOUR PARENTS! •

We're so grateful to your parents for bringing us *you*.

SEEING YOU WITH ONE PARENT, WE LOVE HOW _____

_____

_____

_____

_____

WATCHING YOU WITH YOUR OTHER PARENT MAKES US THINK _____

_____

_____

_____

_____

WE CAN TELL ALREADY THAT YOU AND
YOUR PARENTS HAVE A SPECIAL BOND BECAUSE _____

_____

_____

_____

_____

SPECIAL CEREMONIES

Whether it's a baby-naming ceremony, baptism, bris, or other ceremonial event, traditions create a sense of continuity in a family. And they're a great way to celebrate! Here's a ceremony or tradition we celebrated after your birth.

CEREMONY: _____

DATE AND TIME: _____

PLACE: _____

GUESTS:

_____   _____

_____   _____

_____   _____

_____   _____

_____   _____

REMEMBRANCES OF THE DAY:

_____

_____

_____

_____

PLACE A PHOTO FROM A
SPECIAL CEREMONY HERE.

⊪ ⊪ ⊪ WELCOME TO OUR HOUSE ⊪ ⊪ ⊪

We love sharing our home with you.
Here's how things went the first time you came for a visit.

_____

_____

_____

_____

_____

WHERE WE LIVE: _____

_____

WHAT YOU ATE: _____

_____

THINGS WE DID: _____

_____

OTHER VISITORS: _____

_____

PLACE A PHOTO OF BABY'S FIRST VISIT HERE.

PLACE A PHOTO OF BABY AND GRANDPARENT 1 HERE.

PLACE A PHOTO OF BABY AND GRANDPARENT 2 HERE.

PLACE A PHOTO OF BABY IN THE TUB HERE.

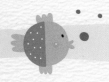

BATH TIME!

Rub-a-dub-dub! Rubber duckies, bubbles, and giggles—there's
nothing more fun than bath time with baby.

**HERE'S A STORY ABOUT THE FIRST
TIME WE GAVE YOU A BATH:**

_____

_____

_____

_____

_____

_____

_____

_____

**HERE'S HOW YOU REACTED TO
BATH TIME:**

_____

_____

_____

**YOUR FAVORITE BATH TOYS AT OUR
HOUSE WERE:**

_____

_____

_____

**YOU LIKED TO PLAY THESE GAMES OR
READ THESE BOOKS IN THE TUB:**

_____

_____

_____

~ READ ALL ABOUT IT ~

It's fun to explore the world of imagination and books together!

HERE IS THE FIRST BOOK WE READ TO YOU:

_____

HERE ARE SOME OTHER FAVORITE BOOKS WE LOVED TO READ TOGETHER:

_____   _____

_____   _____

_____   _____

PLACE A PHOTO OF STORY TIME HERE.

YOUR FAVORITE THINGS

We love watching you explore your world when we're together!
Here are some of your favorite things to do when you're with us.

■ FAVORITE FOODS:

_____

_____

_____

■ FAVORITE GAMES:

_____

_____

_____

■ FAVORITE TOYS:

_____

_____

_____

■ FAVORITE SILLY SONGS:

_____

_____

_____

■ FAVORITE PLAYMATES:

_____

_____

_____

■ OTHER FAVORITE ACTIVITIES:

_____

_____

_____

THE FIRST TIME
WE BABYSAT YOU

Your parents couldn't be home, but they left you in good hands!
Babysitting is a grandparent's rite of passage. Here's how it went when we were in charge.

A LITTLE STORY ABOUT OUR FIRST TIME BABYSITTING YOU:

_____

_____

_____

_____

HERE ARE SOME RULES AND INSTRUCTIONS YOUR PARENTS LEFT
IN THEIR ABSENCE:

_____

_____

_____

_____

SHHH! DON'T TELL YOUR PARENTS THAT WE LET YOU _____

_____

_____

PLACE A PHOTO OF THE EXPERIENCE HERE.

PLACE PHOTOS FROM FAVORITE OUTINGS HERE.

♥ OH, THE PLACES WE GO! ♥

Let's hit the town!
There's a whole wide world out there, and we're excited to explore it together.

HERE'S WHERE WE WENT ON OUR FIRST OUTING TOGETHER,
AND ALL THE FUN WE HAD!

_____

_____

_____

_____

_____

HERE ARE OTHER PLACES WE ENJOY GOING TOGETHER:

_____

_____

_____

_____

_____

YOUR FIRST SLEEPOVER

The good times never end when you sleep over at our house!
Here's what happened at your first sleepover here.

DATE: _____

SPECIAL MEMORIES OF THE BIG EVENT:

_____

_____

_____

_____

_____

_____

PLACE PHOTOS FROM
BABY'S FIRST SLEEPOVER HERE.

MAKE ROOM FOR BABY!

PLACE A PHOTO OF BABY'S CRIB OR BASSINET
AT OUR HOUSE HERE.

✬ BEDTIME ROUTINES WITH BABY ✬

YOUR SPECIAL BEDTIME ROUTINE:

_____

_____

_____

_____

LULLABIES WE SING YOU:

_____

_____

_____

FAVORITE GOOD NIGHT STORIES:

_____

_____

_____

• MOTHER'S DAY •

Mother's Day takes on new meaning when you're a grandmother.
There's something profound about generations gathering
to honor and celebrate motherhood.

HERE'S A STORY ABOUT MY FIRST MOTHER'S DAY AS YOUR GRANDMOTHER:

_____

_____

_____

_____

_____

HERE'S WHAT MOTHER'S DAY MEANS TO ME NOW THAT I'M A GRANDMOTHER:

_____

_____

_____

_____

_____

PLACE MOTHER'S DAY CARD HERE.

• FATHER'S DAY •

Father's Day is fun when you're a dad—and even more special when you're a grandpa.
I'm proud to share this day with generations of fathers in our family.

HERE'S A STORY ABOUT MY FIRST FATHER'S DAY AS YOUR GRANDFATHER:

_____

_____

_____

_____

_____

HERE'S WHAT FATHER'S DAY MEANS TO ME NOW THAT I'M A GRANDFATHER:

_____

_____

_____

_____

_____

PLACE FATHER'S DAY CARD HERE.

FUN IN THE SUN

Sprinklers, sand castles, and sunshine—summer is a time for relaxation and family fun. Here are some of our favorite summer memories with you!

PLACE SUMMERTIME PHOTO HERE.

SPOOKY HALLOWEEN MEMORIES

Boo! What's cuter than a baby in a costume?
Here is a moment from your first Halloween. No tricks here—just lots of treats!

PLACE "SPOOK-TACULAR" HALLOWEEN PHOTO HERE.

THANKSGIVING

We have so much to be grateful for now that you are here.

HERE ARE OUR MEMORIES OF OUR FIRST THANKSGIVING
AS YOUR GRANDPARENTS:

_____

_____

_____

_____

_____

_____

HERE'S WHAT WE'RE GRATEFUL FOR THIS THANKSGIVING:

_____

_____

_____

_____

_____

PLACE THANKSGIVING
PHOTOS HERE.

CELEBRATING WINTER HOLIDAYS

Oh, the weather outside is frightful . . . but moments with you are so delightful.
Here's a look at the first winter holidays we celebrated together.

HOLIDAY(S) WE CELEBRATED: _____

_____

WHERE WE GATHERED: _____

_____

OUR GIFTS TO YOU: _____

_____

OTHER SPECIAL GIFTS YOU RECEIVED: _____

_____

SPECIAL FAMILY HOLIDAY TRADITIONS: _____

_____

HERE ARE MORE MEMORIES OF THE FESTIVITIES:

_____

_____

_____

_____

_____

PLACE WINTER HOLIDAY PHOTOS HERE.

PLACE PHOTOS WITH EXTENDED FAMILY HERE.

⤜ A FAMILY AFFAIR! ⤛

We love seeing you with the rest of the family—aunts, uncles, cousins, and close friends.
Here is a collection of special photographs with other members of the family.

HERE ARE THE NAMES OF YOUR RELATIVES:

- AUNTS

_____

_____

_____

_____

_____

- UNCLES

_____

_____

_____

_____

_____

- COUSINS

_____

_____

_____

_____

- CLOSE FRIENDS

_____

_____

_____

_____

❧ YOUR FIRST BIRTHDAY ❧

We can't believe you're already one! It's been a magical year, filled with the wonder
of first smiles and first glimpses of the world. And now, on your first birthday,
friends and family gather to celebrate sweet, adorable, much-loved you!

HERE IS HOW WE CELEBRATED YOUR FIRST BIRTHDAY:

_____

_____

_____

_____

OUR GIFT(S) TO YOU:

_____

_____

OTHER SPECIAL GIFTS YOU RECEIVED:

_____

_____

_____

PLACE FIRST BIRTHDAY PHOTOS HERE.

HOW WE FEEL SEEING YOU TURN ONE:

_____

_____

_____

_____

_____

HOW YOUR PARENTS HANDLED THE BIG DAY:

_____

_____

_____

_____

_____

_____

We can't believe how much you've grown over the first year!

PLACE PHOTO OF
YOUR ONE-YEAR-OLD GRANDCHILD HERE.

PLACE PHOTOS OF SOME BABY FIRSTS HERE.

⤬ YOUR COLLECTION OF FIRSTS ⤬

Here's a look at some of your important milestones (courtesy of your parents)!

▼ WHEN YOU FIRST SMILED: _____

▼ WHEN YOUR FIRST TOOTH ARRIVED:_____

▼ YOUR FIRST SOLID FOOD: _____

▼ WHEN YOU FIRST CRAWLED: _____

▼ WHEN YOU FIRST STOOD: _____

▼ WHEN YOU TOOK YOUR FIRST STEPS: _____

▼ YOUR FIRST WORD: _____

▼ YOUR FIRST HAIRCUT: _____

▼ OTHER FIRSTS: _____

_____

_____

_____

YOUR SECOND BIRTHDAY

Look at you, you're two!

HERE ARE SPECIAL MEMORIES FROM YOUR SECOND BIRTHDAY:

_____

_____

_____

_____

_____

_____

_____

_____

_____

_____

PLACE SECOND BIRTHDAY PHOTOS HERE.

PLACE THIRD BIRTHDAY
PHOTOS HERE.

YOUR THIRD BIRTHDAY

Yippee! You're three!

HERE'S A STORY FROM YOUR THIRD BIRTHDAY:

_____

_____

_____

_____

_____

_____

_____

_____

_____

_____

_____

❀ NAMES YOU CALL US ❀

What's in a name? Here are your special names for us.

NAME(S) FOR GRANDPARENT 1: _____

_____

NAME(S) FOR GRANDPARENT 2: _____

_____

PLACE PHOTO OF BABY AND GRANDPARENTS HERE.

☆ HOW YOU MAKE US LAUGH ☆

You're a comedian!
Here are some of the ways you bring smiles and laughter to our lives.

_____

_____

_____

_____

_____

_____

_____

_____

_____

_____

_____

_____

_____

OUR QUOTABLE GRANDCHILD

We can't believe some of the things you say!
Here are some of your more memorable quotes from our time together.

"
_____

_____

_____
"

Date: _____

"
_____

_____

_____
"

Date: _____

"
_____

_____

_____
"

Date: _____

"

_____

_____

"

_____

Date: _____

"

_____

_____

"

_____

Date: _____

"

_____

_____

"

_____

Date: _____

"

_____

_____

"

_____

Date: _____

OUR GRANDCHILD, THE ARTIST

We love getting artwork from our talented grandchild. Here are some finger paintings, drawings, and other masterpieces from our favorite artist.

PLACE ARTWORK HERE.

PLACE ARTWORK HERE.

HOW WE SPOIL YOU ROTTEN

One of the best parts of being a grandparent is all the fun stuff you get to
give to and do with your grandchild. Here's how we love to spoil you
(despite your parents' best intentions)!

_____

_____

_____

_____

_____

_____

_____

_____

_____

_____

OUR FASHION MODEL

Onesies, sundresses, and hats, oh my!
Here are photographs of you dressed in clothes from us.

PLACE PHOTOS HERE.

HOW YOU REMIND US OF YOUR PARENTS

Your mother's determination. Your father's laugh.
Here are the ways we see your parents in you.

_____

_____

_____

_____

_____

_____

_____

AND HERE ARE SOME WAYS YOU ARE UNIQUELY _YOU_:

_____

_____

_____

_____

_____

_____

○ THE BEST PART OF ○
BEING A GRANDPARENT

There's so much to love about being a grandparent.
Here are some of the ways being a grandparent has brought joy to our lives.

_____

_____

_____

_____

_____

_____

_____

_____

_____

_____

_____

_____

_____

_____

YOUR NOTE TO US!

Here's a note or special drawing you made just for us!

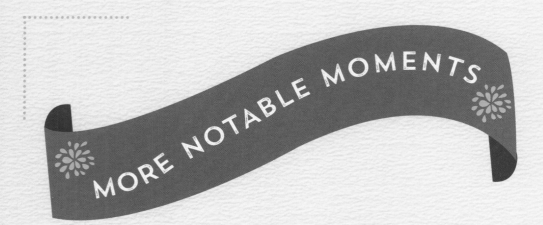

MORE NOTABLE MOMENTS

PHOTO ALBUM